GCSE English Language
Revise Non-Fiction Writing
Sample Answers and Practice
from
GCSEEnglish.uk

Edward Mooney

gcseenglish.uk

2020

First Printing: 2020

ISBN 979-8-550-95316-7

www.gcseenglish.uk

Contents

Introduction

I wrote this selection of model exam answers to help my students prepare for their GCSE English Language exams and I am publishing them here so that you too can use them to improve your exam grades.

In your GCSE English Language exams, the non-fiction task will count for between 17% and 30% of total marks awarded (depending on the exam board) so practising non-fiction writing is absolutely vital and can make a huge difference to your final grades.

What is non-fiction writing?

Each exam board gives non-fiction writing a slightly different name so you may know it as:

- writing to present a viewpoint
- persuasive writing
- transactional writing
- directed writing.

There are some differences in the way each exam board sets the non-fiction task but, to a great extent, what is required is the same: a continuous piece of non-fiction writing in which you present a viewpoint on an issue and demonstrate excellent contemporary Standard English.

For more information on exam board differences (especially timing and mark percentages) please see Appendix 1 at the end of the book.

How will my writing be assessed?

Exam boards will assess your writing against two Assessment Objectives:

AO5	Communicate clearly, effectively and imaginatively, selecting and adapting tone, style and register for different forms, purposes and audiences. Organise information and ideas, using structural and grammatical features to support coherence and cohesion of texts.
AO6	Candidates must use a range of vocabulary and sentence structures for clarity, purpose and effect, with accurate spelling and punctuation.

This exam board language, however, can feel a bit vague. After all, what does "coherence and cohesion" mean? Who decides what is "effective" and what isn't?

(Answers: coherence means that your text should make sense as a whole – the reader should understand clearly what's going on. Cohesion means your sentences should follow the normal rules of Standard English written grammar. It is your examiner, ultimately, who will decide what is effective and what isn't.)

Rather than answering these questions theoretically, the texts in this book aim to show in practical terms how it's possible to give your examiner what they are looking for, within the time constraints of the exam, whilst also showing off the full range of your creativity and writing technique.

What makes these excellent exam answers?

The twelve texts here show how you can make good decisions about tone, style and register in order to write a text in the required form identified in the wording of the exam task (article, letter, speech). The texts present the required viewpoints by interweaving factual information and emotive language, and by building to a powerful ending. They are effective and compelling texts that examiners would reward with high marks.

The texts also showcase the accurate spelling, consistent punctuation and clear grammar that the examiners are expecting.

Moreover, these texts are short – no more than 750 words. The first drafts were written under the same conditions as the ones you will face (45 minutes for the AQA exam) and therefore reflect what is possible in such a short time.

How to use this book

There are a range of different ways you can use this book. You could:

- read the texts and see what an excellent exam answer looks like.
- read the exam task and then plan and write your own text.
- use the checklists (provided after every text) to see how many of the writing recommendations are met by each text.
- use the checklists (provided after every text) to help you plan and write your own texts.
- read the texts again, more slowly, identifying key language features (e.g. rhetorical questions, powerful use of personal pronouns, emotive language, tricolon).
- re-write the texts to present a different viewpoint (especially if you disagree with the viewpoint here!).

Of course, these are practice tasks and model answers. Your writing in your exam should be your own work. Don't attempt to memorise a text and copy it out as you risk being penalised, such as having marks taken away or even being disqualified from the entire exam.

Statistics, quotations from experts, footnotes

As the topic of the text you are asked to write is not communicated before the exam, it is not possible to learn statistics or quotations from experts beforehand. Instead, I recommend using your general knowledge and common sense to help you craft plausible statistics and quotations.

In the texts in this book, the experts are invented. Each is given a title, a name and a workplace and then they offer two to three useful snippets of information which are presented in quotation marks.

The data used in these texts, however, is real and comes from a range of online sources. Like all data, it is liable to change and re-interpretation. Future editions of this book will endeavour to update data, as and when new sources become available.

Clearly, as you will not be able to do research in an exam, footnotes are not expected by examiners. However, I include them here should you want to follow up any of the ideas and find some useful data for your own texts.

A clickable list of references is available at: https://gcseenglish.uk/non-fiction-references.

More about me

I am a qualified teacher of English with a degree in English Literature from the University of Cambridge. I have taught and examined GCSE and A Level English courses at outstanding schools since 2006. I now tutor students online through my website gcseenglish.uk.

Read reviews and keep up to date with future projects and more exam guidance by subscribing to my social media channels. Search gcseenglishuk and feel free to leave a review.

I hope you enjoy reading these texts and find them useful in improving your own non-fiction and, who knows, you may one day write the next bestseller!

Best of luck in your exams!

1: An article about homework

You are advised to spend the correct amount of time on this section (check Appendix 1 for your exam board's time).
Write in full sentences.
You are reminded of the need to plan your answer.
You should leave enough time to check your work at the end.

"Homework has no value. Some students get it done for them; some don't do it at all. Students should be relaxing in their free time."

Write an article for a broadsheet newspaper in which you explain your point of view on this statement.

Space for planning:

1: The Text

Homework is at crisis point. Teachers set too much or not enough whilst students either refuse to do it, do it badly or throw money at the problem by outsourcing their work to dark web essay cheats. We risk, therefore, losing sight of the purpose of homework: to broaden and deepen knowledge and to practise and perfect skills. Instead, it is seen by many as an anachronistic burden that gets in the way of rest and relaxation, detrimental to both mental and physical health. But does it have to be this way? With a little re-imagining, homework can be made fit for purpose, helping young people to be their best selves and to achieve their goals in an increasingly competitive global marketplace.

On average, students in the UK receive five hours of homework per week. However, this average rises significantly as exams approach. Including time spent in lessons and other school-related activities, an average student will spend close to 50 hours per week on their education.[1] This is far more than the 39 hours per week an average adult works.[2] No wonder then that OFSTED surveys show that homework is a major cause of stress.[3] It doesn't seem right that children are burdened with more work and more stress than adults. Something must change.

Yet, whilst complaining about homework has a long history, it remains stubbornly part of the education system. As far back as 1900, it was referred to as a "national crime" which "rob[s] a child of...playtime," by American campaigner Edward Bok. Nevertheless, homework flourished, driven at least partly by parents who argued in favour of heavy workloads. The Cold War also led to increased pressure as, especially in the USA, fears that millions of hardworking Soviet school children would soon outstrip the 'lazy' American student led teachers to fill playtime with ever more homework.[4] In the USA then, as elsewhere, parents, teachers and politicians can't seem to agree. Either homework is idealised, or it is demonised. Is there a solution to this impasse?

[1] Chris Morris and School Reporters, *BBC News*, 15 March 2018.
[2] Debra Leaker, *Office for National Statistics*, August 2020.
[3] Eleanor Busby, *The Independent*, 19 March 2018.
[4] Rebecca Onion, *Slate*, 24 October 2019.

Perhaps we can learn from the experience of Janine, a school student from Swaffham. Two years ago, her exams fast approaching, her workload rising, she stopped doing homework set by teachers and instead decided to choose her own homework. She began learning Spanish on Duolingo, watching maths tutorials on YouTube and reading widely. Her teachers and parents despaired but they needn't have. Janine sat her exams better prepared and less stressed than many of her peers and consequently her grades were excellent; she even made it to the front page of the local paper. This solution might not work for all – it requires initiative, discipline and a strong desire to learn – but it worked for Janine so why not for others?

Some dismiss these suggestions as nonsense and contend that homework is key, pointing to the long hours at many private schools as evidence that hard graft leads to success. Indeed, the numbers appear to bear this out. A 2014 Department for Education report concluded that Year 9s who spend between two and three hours on homework per night are almost 10 times more likely to achieve five good GCSEs than students who did no homework at all.[5] The report, however, makes no reference to the quality of the work. Many students can point to homework tasks they believe to be a pointless time-fillers and ask how helpful those tasks are to their future exam success or, indeed, to their future lives.

Perhaps, then, the solution is not to ban homework, nor even to set less homework. Instead, teachers need to design better homework that feels meaningful, is clearly assessment focused and possibly even allows some independent choice. Moreover, teachers should leverage all the possibilities of the internet to connect their students to knowledge and to ways of learning unavailable to them in the classroom. After all, long gone are the days when the height of learning technology was a slate and a piece of chalk. Ultimately, if students feel that their homework is not just a confiscation of their free time but instead an opportunity to broaden their understanding and improve readiness for exams, and for life, then there will surely be more buy-in from today's busy, stressed teens.

[5] Chris Morris and School Reporters, *BBC News*, 15 March 2018.

1: Writing Checklist

As you read, check how many of the recommendations below are followed by the text. Then, use the checklist to help you write your own text.

Remember that these are *recommendations* from an experienced teacher, not *requirements*. Allow them to help and guide you, but don't allow them to trap you; if you have a different idea and feel confident and excited about it, then give it a go!

- ☐ Clearly meets the purpose of the task.
- ☐ Clearly communicates to the audience of the task.
- ☐ Clearly meets the requested format of the task.
- ☐ Five to six main paragraphs.
- ☐ Structured to lead to a powerful 'call to action' closing.
- ☐ Range of different styles: descriptive, factual, emotive.
- ☐ Use of specific detail (avoiding vagueness and repetition).
- ☐ Five to seven sentences per paragraph.
- ☐ Sentences are varied lengths.
- ☐ Use of fronted adverbial.
- ☐ Use of extended noun phrase.

- ☐ Vocabulary is more formal than everyday language.
- ☐ Contains descriptive language.
- ☐ Contains facts.
- ☐ Contains statistics.
- ☐ Contains quotations.
- ☐ Contains a small number of rhetorical questions.
- ☐ No overuse or repetition of "I."
- ☐ Powerful, non-repetitive use of "we" and/or "you."
- ☐ Spelling, punctuation and grammar are accurate.
- ☐ Use of: colon, semi-colon, hyphen, dash.
- ☐ 450-750 words in total.

2: A letter about music festivals

You are advised to spend the correct amount of time on this section (check Appendix 1 for your exam board's time).
Write in full sentences.
You are reminded of the need to plan your answer.
You should leave enough time to check your work at the end.

"Festivals and fairs should be banned. They encourage bad behaviour and are disruptive to local communities."

Write a letter to your local newspaper in which you argue for or against this statement.

Space for planning:

2: The Text

Dear Madam,

Last week, you printed an excited preview of Rocksham music festival. However, we the residents of Repham St Mary, would like you and your readers to consider for a moment the less-than-positive impacts of the festival. Our green and pleasant fields are transformed into a sea of mud, our quiet country lanes are clogged with traffic whilst cacophonic music and the rumble of a thousand diesel generators blight our lives. Then, when the crowds leave, we gaze out over an apocalypse of rubbish: empty beer cans, collapsed tents, discarded wellies. It doesn't have to be like this, and we'd like to take the time to suggest improvements to the running of the festival that will benefit us all.

It is undeniably true that the festival pumps much needed money into the local economy. According to UK Music, the average spend by each 'music tourist' is £850 and last year Rocksham generated £31m profit. [6,7] Yet, how much of that money stays here in the community? Many of the locally recruited festival workers receive tickets and a T-shirt in lieu of salary. This exploitative labour practice would be illegal in any other industry. Similarly, many family-owned businesses shut during the festival because of the security lockdown, losing two weeks of high season revenue. Surely the revellers who flock to Rocksham would be appalled to hear that their joy means the ruin of others?

Last year, local blogger Alyssa Pargeter's exposé on festival life at Rocksham found "something very different from the Instagram images of happy teenagers that adorn festival publicity." She documented illegal drugs being sold and consumed openly and saw people collapsed from drunkenness being revived by over-worked and harassed medical staff. She investigated gangs of thieves moving from tent to tent. Most harrowing was her discussion of the levels of sexual assault during the festivals she visited, much of which, she notes, goes un-punished. "This is the untold story of festival life," she argues. "How long can we allow this to happen?" Clearly, we need to find a way to run festivals and minimise harm to festival goers and local residents.

[6] Natalie Williams, *UK Music*, 2017.
[7] Profit for the invented Rocksham Festival based on Reading Festival: Rahul Vashisht, *Berkshire Live*, 8 March 2015.

Solutions are easy to find. Rock na Cloiche festival in the west of Ireland is a similar sized event yet has none of the issues we feel are problems for Rocksham. The organisers employ local people at all levels, including using local vendors in their supply chain. They pay attractive wages and contribute to employees' pensions whilst music technology and project management apprenticeships for school leavers are funded from festival profits. Local roads have been widened and re-laid using funds from the festival organisers and a fleet of electric buses transports attendees to the site. During the rest of the year, those same buses transport children to school right across the county. We urge the organisers of Rocksham to consider taking similar steps.

As regards improving behaviour and safety at the festival, we encourage the festival organisers to work more closely with the local constabulary to co-ordinate efforts. Crime can be tackled by deploying dummy surveillance tents, CCTV and visible police patrols. The supply lines of illegal drugs onto the site can be disrupted by gathering intelligence and using it in a timely manner. Drunkenness can be moderated through greater emphasis on providing low-alcohol beverages. To that end, the festival should fund social media campaigns aimed at celebrating sobriety rather than inebriation. Most importantly, the festival should declare a zero tolerance attitude to violence and work with local stakeholders to develop a better response to reports of sexual assault. No one should feel unsafe at Rocksham.

Festivals and fairs have a long and glorious history and in Repham St Mary we love what a well-run festival can be: exciting, colourful, life-changing. We would never argue that the festival be banned. However, we hope that you and your readers understand that there has to be a balance between the desires of the festivalgoers, the profit margins of the organisers and the lives of the people who live in the community for the other 360 days of the year. We believe our recommendations strike that balance. We look forward to further contact with the organisers as we work together to make Rocksham a beacon to the world and the best that a festival can be.

Yours faithfully,

Eliza Cavell.

(Mayor of Repham St Mary)

2: Writing Checklist

As you read, check how many of the recommendations below are followed by the text. Then, use the checklist to help you write your own text.

Remember that these are *recommendations* from an experienced teacher, not *requirements*. Allow them to help and guide you, but don't allow them to trap you; if you have a different idea and feel confident and excited about it, then give it a go!

☐ Clearly meets the purpose of the task.

☐ Clearly communicates to the audience of the task.

☐ Clearly meets the requested format of the task.

☐ Five to six main paragraphs.

☐ Structured to lead to a powerful 'call to action' closing.

☐ Range of different styles: descriptive, factual, emotive.

☐ Use of specific detail (avoiding vagueness and repetition).

☐ Five to seven sentences per paragraph.

☐ Sentences are varied lengths.

☐ Use of fronted adverbial.

☐ Use of extended noun phrase.

☐ Vocabulary is more formal than everyday language.

☐ Contains descriptive language.

☐ Contains facts.

☐ Contains statistics.

☐ Contains quotations.

☐ Contains a small number of rhetorical questions.

☐ No overuse or repetition of "I."

☐ Powerful, non-repetitive use of "we" and/or "you."

☐ Spelling, punctuation and grammar are accurate.

☐ Use of: colon, semi-colon, hyphen, dash.

☐ 450-750 words in total.

3: A speech about the environment

You are advised to spend the correct amount of time on this section (check Appendix 1 for your exam board's time).
Write in full sentences.
You are reminded of the need to plan your answer.
You should leave enough time to check your work at the end.

"Floods, earthquakes, hurricanes and landslides – we see more and more reports of environmental disasters affecting the world and its people every day."

Write the text of a speech for a debate at your school or college in which you persuade young people to take more responsibility for protecting the environment.

Space for planning:

3: The Text

Ladies and gentlemen, we are on the front line of climate change. Our school, when it was built in 1922, was over a mile from the North Sea. Then came the devastating floods of 1953 that claimed hundreds of lives and inundated farmland for miles around, after which, sea defences were built. But the sea kept coming and now, the school teeters precariously on a crumbling cliff only yards from the crashing waves – next winter might be our last. We need to stop procrastinating and grasp the nettle now. We cannot wait for others to step in and solve our problems. It falls to us to stand up and make the changes necessary to put a halt to the devastation of climate change.

We are not alone in facing the crisis of rising sea levels. In The Netherlands, famously low-lying, plans are being drawn up to strengthen the already eye-wateringly expensive Delta Works defences at an estimated cost of £90.5bn.[8] Few nations can afford to dump so much concrete into the sea. By 2050, with sea levels in the Bay of Bengal projected to rise by as much as 50cm, 15 million Bangladeshis will have their lives turned upside down by the ever-encroaching sea.[9] Families will face the agonising decision to pack up and seek higher land. The problem we have here in Norfolk is: we don't have any higher land. What are we to do?

Moreover, sea level rise is only one effect of climate change. Changing agricultural practices during the 20th Century produced more food to feed an exploding world population.[10] Indeed, the share of the population who are undernourished has therefore fallen to historically low levels, though there is further work to do to eradicate hunger.[11] But this dramatic expansion of agricultural yields has come at what cost? Artificial fertiliser runs off into watercourses, destroying delicate ecosystems. Chemicals protect the crops but kill insects and diesel is burnt by the barrel-load in farm machinery.[12] We have

---

[8] *The New York Times*, 3 September 2008.
[9] *Environmental Justice Foundation*, 29 May 2018.
[10] Max Roser, *Our World in Data*, 2014.
[11] Max Roser and Hannah Ritchie, *Our World in Data*, 2013.
[12] Hannah Ritchie, *Our World in Data*, 4 November 2019.

to find better, cleaner, ways to produce food for a projected world population of 11 billion people by 2100.[13]

Now, after such a litany of bad news, allow me to posit some recommendations. No more development should be planned for flood plains or vulnerable coastlines without careful thought given to water management. Upland areas should be 're-wilded' to allow them to trap and slowly release rainfall in a more natural way rather than allowing water to plummet in concrete culverts down into our vulnerable cities and towns. Water retention ponds should be dug to protect our built environment and to serve simultaneously as places for wildlife to thrive. Sandscaping along our coastlines can help mitigate the effects of storm surges, protecting cliff edges from ever more erosion. However, these steps only serve to counter the effects of environmental degradation. What about the causes?

To get at the causes, we need to think more long term. All of us should consider focusing much more on our science education because it is we who will be at the forefront of devising scientific and technological solutions to our over-reliance on carbon and our outrageous disregard for nature. Yet, enrolment on hard science courses at A Level and higher is dropping. We need to step up, take those exams and be the engineers who change the world for the better. Work is happening right now on developing nuclear fusion technology, designing new construction techniques and researching carbon capture systems. We could be a part of that and, if you need more persuading, the pay isn't bad either.

I realise that these steps are difficult. In some cases, they are expensive, and it may be our children who reap the reward of such hard work. However, we need to resist the siren call of short-term patch-and-mend solutions. We should be worried, but we should also be clear-sighted and strong. History shows us that humans have the capacity to do great damage. History also shows us that when we choose to, we are really good at solving problems and making the world a better place. Not for nothing have we given ourselves the rather flattering name homo sapiens, the wise human. Let's live up to that name and build a better future, starting now.

[13] *Environmental Justice Foundation*, 29 May 2018.

3: Writing Checklist

As you read, check how many of the recommendations below are followed by the text. Then, use the checklist to help you write your own text.

Remember that these are *recommendations* from an experienced teacher, not *requirements*. Allow them to help and guide you, but don't allow them to trap you; if you have a different idea and feel confident and excited about it, then give it a go!

☐ Clearly meets the purpose of the task.

☐ Clearly communicates to the audience of the task.

☐ Clearly meets the requested format of the task.

☐ Five to six main paragraphs.

☐ Structured to lead to a powerful 'call to action' closing.

☐ Range of different styles: descriptive, factual, emotive.

☐ Use of specific detail (avoiding vagueness and repetition).

☐ Five to seven sentences per paragraph.

☐ Sentences are varied lengths.

☐ Use of fronted adverbial.

☐ Use of extended noun phrase.

☐ Vocabulary is more formal than everyday language.

☐ Contains descriptive language.

☐ Contains facts.

☐ Contains statistics.

☐ Contains quotations.

☐ Contains a small number of rhetorical questions.

☐ No overuse or repetition of "I."

☐ Powerful, non-repetitive use of "we" and/or "you."

☐ Spelling, punctuation and grammar are accurate.

☐ Use of: colon, semi-colon, hyphen, dash.

☐ 450-750 words in total.

4: An article about adventurous activities

You are advised to spend the correct amount of time on this section (check Appendix 1 for your exam board's time).
Write in full sentences.
You are reminded of the need to plan your answer.
You should leave enough time to check your work at the end.

"Parents today are over-protective. They should let their children take part in adventurous, even risky, activities to prepare them for later life."

Write an article for a broadsheet newspaper in which you argue for or against this statement.

Space for planning:

4: The Text

Twenty-first century parents hover permanently over their children, ready at a moment's notice to intervene. These helicopter parents fret endlessly about all the possible, though highly improbable, negative outcomes in any situation. They buy plastic goggles so their six-year-old can play conkers. They veto a school trip to a climbing wall because they fear loss of life and limb and they install listening apps on their children's phones so they can track their child in real time. It is true that these children are at risk but not in the way their parents think. Instead, they are at risk of growing up into timid, risk-averse adults who will struggle to cope with life's complex challenges. Are modern parents raising a generation of the faint-hearted?

Surveys repeatedly show that time spent by children in unsupervised play has plummeted. Adults from older generations often look back happily on long summer days staying out until sunset. A modern-day child is more likely to be inside with a screen under the watchful gaze of a parent. In fact, according to a 2016 report in The Guardian, "three quarters of UK children spend less time outside than prison inmates."[14] A recent government report notes that 12% of children never visit the natural environment.[15] The kinds of adventurous, even risky activities that were once central to an upbringing are being denied our children.

One young adult who believes that his life has been scarred by over-protection in his youth is Rhodri, a recent university graduate. Carefully mollycoddled well into his teenage years, he struggled when he left home for the freedom of university. "I went off the rails and made lots of foolish decisions." Simply first year high jinks? "It was worse than just letting off steam though," says Rhodri. "One day, I was found at dawn fifty miles from home. I had no idea how I got there." Was he drunk? "No," says Rhodri. "I just started walking and kept going until I dropped. I think it was a cry for help." Counselling has helped Rhodri develop a more thoughtful attitude to risk and he feels more able now to make better decisions about when to take risks and when to avoid them.

[14] Damian Carrington, *The Guardian*, March 25 2016.
[15] A. Hunt, D. Stewart, J. Burt and J. Dillon, *Natural England*, 10 Feb 2016.

In Switzerland, adventure is central to how the nation perceives itself and therefore Swiss parents are much more likely to allow their children to take part in risky activities. Participation in downhill skiing is common meaning some children will spend their weekends reaching speeds of 75km/h on icy slopes with only some red netting to protect them. Parascending, rock climbing, and canyoning are everyday activities for young Swiss people. One Briton who has embraced the Swiss attitude is Anastasia Brajovic, who in 2015 at the age of 13, climbed the 4478m peak of the Matterhorn.[16] Anastasia faced her fears, set her mind to a challenge, understood the risks and succeeded.

It is true, of course, that accidents do happen. On the other hand, a child is unlikely to break their femur when playing with their phone, no matter how strenuous the game of Angry Birds gets. However, the statistics show that for the vast majority, engagement in adventure activities is just that: an adventure. There is a vanishingly small risk of death from skiing for example (0.00007%) and comparably small risks for other adventure activities.[17] An inactive lifestyle, on the other hand, though safe in the short term may actually be storing up trouble for the future as it is argued that people who are overweight or obese are more likely to die earlier.[18]

So, parents of the UK, take a step back and relax. Let your loved ones grow into capable adults the way you did: by taking risks, by making mistakes and by learning from them. The future is always uncertain and the best way to prepare for it is to be resilient, thoughtful and capable. A new generation who are as au fait with karabiners, skateboards and OS maps as they are with their own four walls may well be the first generation to live off Earth in a Mars pod, whiling away their free time skiing down Olympus Mons. The 21st Century is exciting – don't turn away from it. Allow your children, and yourselves, to embrace adventure and see where it takes you!

[16] *SWNS*, 9 September 2015.
[17] *Teton Gravity Research*, 24 July 2019.
[18] *NHS*, 14 July 2016.

4: Writing Checklist

As you read, check how many of the recommendations below are followed by the text. Then, use the checklist to help you write your own text.

Remember that these are *recommendations* from an experienced teacher, not *requirements*. Allow them to help and guide you, but don't allow them to trap you; if you have a different idea and feel confident and excited about it, then give it a go!

☐ Clearly meets the purpose of the task.

☐ Clearly communicates to the audience of the task.

☐ Clearly meets the requested format of the task.

☐ Five to six main paragraphs.

☐ Structured to lead to a powerful 'call to action' closing.

☐ Range of different styles: descriptive, factual, emotive.

☐ Use of specific detail (avoiding vagueness and repetition).

☐ Five to seven sentences per paragraph.

☐ Sentences are varied lengths.

☐ Use of fronted adverbial.

☐ Use of extended noun phrase.

☐ Vocabulary is more formal than everyday language.

☐ Contains descriptive language.

☐ Contains facts.

☐ Contains statistics.

☐ Contains quotations.

☐ Contains a small number of rhetorical questions.

☐ No overuse or repetition of "I."

☐ Powerful, non-repetitive use of "we" and/or "you."

☐ Spelling, punctuation and grammar are accurate.

☐ Use of: colon, semi-colon, hyphen, dash.

☐ 450-750 words in total.

5: A speech about education

You are advised to spend the correct amount of time on this section (check Appendix 1 for your exam board's time).
Write in full sentences.
You are reminded of the need to plan your answer.
You should leave enough time to check your work at the end.

"Education is not just about which school you go to, or what qualifications you gain; it is also about what you learn from your experiences outside of school."

Write a speech for your school or college Leavers' Day to explain what you think makes a good education.

Space for planning:

5: The Text

Esteemed guests, valued teachers, kind friends, good afternoon.

The time has come for us to fly the nest. We have had many nervous, erratic practice flights, moving tentatively, inexorably, further and further into the great world that lies before us. But now, now we are on our own. There will be times over the coming years when we will get lost but we can take heart that we have been well-prepared and well-educated for the challenges that await us. We may pause and wonder though, on this, the final day of our school lives: how did we get here? What is the obscure process by which we grew from toddlers with permanent scabs on our knees to articulate, knowledgeable, effective adults, ready to work and ready to take on the world? What is, in effect, a good education?

Naturally, what happens in school is vital to our education. We have been lucky enough to attend an outstanding school with hard-working teachers, excellent facilities and an ethos that encourages discipline and risk-taking. But not everyone is so lucky. There are schools where asbestos creates no-go zones and damp rises from the dark earth. There are schools where teachers are overworked, where disruptive behaviour is shrugged at, and exam results slide ever-downwards. Increased funding is part of the answer to these problems and empowering headteachers to deal sternly with poor behaviour of students can only help too. However, although we have spent a large proportion of our lives in school, it represents only part of our education.

A good education needs to move beyond the classroom. Nations such as France and Switzerland offer a baccalaureate qualification which acknowledges the role of creativity and community service in education. Alongside grades gained from academic exams, students are rewarded for commitment to community service and creative arts projects. However, even where there isn't an intrinsic reward for such activity, we have a lot to gain from life outside the classroom. Working to put on a play teaches us responsibility, timekeeping and memorisation, as well as softer skills such as social interaction and teamwork. Taking up a volunteer role in a care home can help us to connect with the older generation, whom we all risk dismissing too readily and from whom we all have much to learn.

There is another set of skills that schools are not best placed to teach us: making and managing money. Yes, you may know all the French irregular verbs, or how to classify amino acids, but can you do a fourteen-hour shift at an aluminium factory? Saturday jobs used to be a common rite of passage for teenagers, but they have fallen out of favour in recent years. However, the discipline and the rigours of the workplace are very rarely replicated in schools. Moreover, the mind-blowing complexity of payslips, National Insurance, emergency tax codes and workplace pensions needs to be lived to be properly understood. So, I will see you this Saturday in Greggs on the High Street and I will tear the little strips off my payslip and feel proud that I am making my way in the world like my parents before me.

This is an end, but it is also a beginning. Education never stops. There will be life lessons, learnt the hard way perhaps, but learnt nonetheless. Many of us will become parents and wonder, in the dead of night, waiting for the milk to warm, how it's even possible to look after these wriggling bundles of noise and smells and possibility. Then the cycle will begin again as we pass on what we have learnt to our children. Even in our autumn years, the work of life done, and done well, we may make the surprising decision to learn the bass guitar, taking lessons beamed by hologram from a teenager in Osaka. Our grandchildren, sitting all fingers and thumbs at the kitchen table, trying to do their maths homework, might be embarrassed, or they might be proud. And we will show them that education is everywhere and for all time.

We have been given the best of starts, the best of educations. Thank you to our teachers and to all involved in building this successful learning community. It falls to us now. We must take up the baton, forge ahead and repay the investment made in us. Good luck, farewell and never stop learning.

5: Writing Checklist

As you read, check how many of the recommendations below are followed by the text. Then, use the checklist to help you write your own text.

Remember that these are *recommendations* from an experienced teacher, not *requirements*. Allow them to help and guide you, but don't allow them to trap you; if you have a different idea and feel confident and excited about it, then give it a go!

☐ Clearly meets the purpose of the task.

☐ Clearly communicates to the audience of the task.

☐ Clearly meets the requested format of the task.

☐ Five to six main paragraphs.

☐ Structured to lead to a powerful 'call to action' closing.

☐ Range of different styles: descriptive, factual, emotive.

☐ Use of specific detail (avoiding vagueness and repetition).

☐ Five to seven sentences per paragraph.

☐ Sentences are varied lengths.

☐ Use of fronted adverbial.

☐ Use of extended noun phrase.

☐ Vocabulary is more formal than everyday language.

☐ Contains descriptive language.

☐ Contains facts.

☐ Contains statistics.

☐ Contains quotations.

☐ Contains a small number of rhetorical questions.

☐ No overuse or repetition of "I."

☐ Powerful, non-repetitive use of "we" and/or "you."

☐ Spelling, punctuation and grammar are accurate.

☐ Use of: colon, semi-colon, hyphen, dash.

☐ 450-750 words in total.

6: An article about corruption in sport

You are advised to spend the correct amount of time on this section (check Appendix 1 for your exam board's time).
Write in full sentences.
You are reminded of the need to plan your answer.
You should leave enough time to check your work at the end.

"All sport should be fun, fair and open to everyone. These days, sport seems to be more about money, corruption and winning at any cost."

Write an article for a newspaper in which you explain your point of view on this statement.

Space for planning:

6: The Text

The cyclist speeds through France at 50 kilometres an hour. The bike is sleek, titanium, 6.8kg and wind-tunnel engineered by top scientists to squeeze every last marginal gain out of its design.[19] The cyclist's chest is emblazoned with sponsorship logos from the world's richest corporations. When he reaches for nourishment, he does not eat 'food'. He squeezes personalised gels into his body, more astronaut than athlete. But what is inside that body, hiding from the gaze of anti-doping organisations? What chemicals course through his muscles and triple the size of his thighs? Is that even his blood? In disgust, we turn away. This is not sport. This is televised corruption.

"Sport needs to be fun, fair and open to everyone." So says Professor Caitlín Ní Riagáin in her recent report on sports participation in the UK. She does not dismiss elite sport out of hand as, she argues, "following the careers of sporting heroes can spur increased sports participation." However, there is a tipping point. "My research shows that many people don't feel able to emulate elite sports stars." Add to that a whiff of corruption, and the high profile of elite athletes can actually have a negative effect on sports participation. "Cynicism sets in," Ní Riagáin notes, "and all our good intentions die. 25% of people in England are 'inactive' according to recent studies."[20]

Myleene was one of that stubborn 25%. She used to spend her days sitting in a seafront bus shelter, munching on crisps, scrolling through YouTube videos showing the impossible lives of the impossibly beautiful. Myleene knew she was hurting herself through inactivity and poor diet, but she'd still go with her friends to the park where they'd down huge bottles of cider. Then she decided that something had to change so she stopped drinking and started running everywhere. It wasn't easy but when she started documenting her journey on social media, she was encouraged by messages of support from all over the world. Suddenly, she was an inspiration to millions and all without corruption or doping. "Adrenaline is my drug," she now says as she speeds off on yet another half marathon.

---

[19] Carlton Reid, *Forbes*, 11 August 2020.
[20] *Sport England*, 23 April 2020.

One success story is not enough though. The government needs to act now to enable millions more to get outdoors and get moving. The English Premier League made £0.9bn in the 2017-2018 football season.[21] By comparison, the annual running costs of a grassroots football club are c£2500.[22] Just think of the stunning facilities and the highly-trained coaches that could be funded by the EPL. Other sporting facilities are sorely lacking. Cycling facilities in the UK are often laughable and can be deadly: 102 cyclists were killed on Britain's roads in 2016.[23] Joined-up thinking is needed to put provision of world-class sports facilities front and centre of any new urban development.

However, sport has another problem. It is presented in the media as the preserve of young, hyper-fit men, turning away those who do not see themselves represented. Moreover, sport finds it difficult to hide the fact that it is hard and liable to make participants smelly and dirty. Image-conscious teens are unlikely to take up an activity that threatens their 'Instagrammability'.[24] Small changes to the attitudes of media writers and opinion formers are needed and could have tremendous positive effects. Imagine an aspirational character in a hit prime time soap who is presented as taking time every day to run five km or to cycle to work. Such a campaign normalises physical activity, suggesting it can be a part of everyone's lives without needing expensive equipment or large amounts of free time.

The situation hangs in the balance. We could look forward to a future where sport is increasingly seen as a passive television experience. Or, with the right policies, funding and changes in behaviour, we may see whole generations convinced of the value of sport for their bodies and their minds. By making physical activity a part of their routines now, the younger generation can look forward to long healthy lives. Every day there is another story about an older person performing some sort of sporting feat. In June 2019, Mavis Paterson, 81, cycled the 906 miles from Land's End to John O'Groats – no drugs, no bungs, no dodgy doctors.[25] Now that's a vision of sport we can all get behind.

[21] *Deloitte*, 25 April 2019.
[22] Oli Brierley, *Kitlocker*, 26 September 2017.
[23] Joël Reland, *Full Fact*, 17 August 2018.
[24] *This Girl Can*.
[25] *BBC News*, 22 June 2019.

6: Writing Checklist

As you read, check how many of the recommendations below are followed by the text. Then, use the checklist to help you write your own text.

Remember that these are *recommendations* from an experienced teacher, not *requirements*. Allow them to help and guide you, but don't allow them to trap you; if you have a different idea and feel confident and excited about it, then give it a go!

- ☐ Clearly meets the purpose of the task.
- ☐ Clearly communicates to the audience of the task.
- ☐ Clearly meets the requested format of the task.
- ☐ Five to six main paragraphs.
- ☐ Structured to lead to a powerful 'call to action' closing.
- ☐ Range of different styles: descriptive, factual, emotive.
- ☐ Use of specific detail (avoiding vagueness and repetition).
- ☐ Five to seven sentences per paragraph.
- ☐ Sentences are varied lengths.
- ☐ Use of fronted adverbial.
- ☐ Use of extended noun phrase.

- ☐ Vocabulary is more formal than everyday language.
- ☐ Contains descriptive language.
- ☐ Contains facts.
- ☐ Contains statistics.
- ☐ Contains quotations.
- ☐ Contains a small number of rhetorical questions.
- ☐ No overuse or repetition of "I."
- ☐ Powerful, non-repetitive use of "we" and/or "you."
- ☐ Spelling, punctuation and grammar are accurate.
- ☐ Use of: colon, semi-colon, hyphen, dash.
- ☐ 450-750 words in total.

7: A letter about cars

You are advised to spend the correct amount of time on this section (check Appendix 1 for your exam board's time).
Write in full sentences.
You are reminded of the need to plan your answer.
You should leave enough time to check your work at the end.

"Cars are noisy, dirty, smelly and downright dangerous. They should be banned from all town and city centres, allowing people to walk and cycle in peace."

Write a letter to the Minister for Transport arguing your point of view on this statement.

Space for planning:

7: The Text

Dear Grant Shapps,

Our cities are in crisis. Every day, young children walk to school along main roads clogged with vehicles pumping poisons and dark smoke out into the atmosphere. Older people live with chronic breathing problems caused by a lifetime of exposure to motor vehicle pollution. In some parts of our cities, people resort to wearing masks to protect their delicate lungs from invasion by hydrocarbon specks that burrow their way insidiously into our bodies and cause cancer. There is only one reasonable course of action: you must ban these agents of disease from our town and city centres.

According to the RAC Foundation, there are 31.7 million cars on Britain's roads and this number grows on average by 610 thousand per annum.[26] Each car pumps out a range of noxious pollutants such as nitrogen oxides (NO_x) and particulate matter (PM_{10} and $PM_{2.5}$). Couple this with the fact that poor air quality reduces average UK life expectancy at birth by six months and you have an entirely avoidable public health crisis on your hands. According to the RAC, the cost of this pollution to human health is "estimated at between £4.5bn and £10bn annually to the UK economy."[27] You will agree, I am sure, that this money could clearly be put to better use.

Pollution is not the only problem caused by motor vehicles. Take Will for instance. Will was leading a happy life, working hard running a prosperous local business and bringing up his three children. Sadly, one day, his world was turned upside down. A driver, distracted by her mobile phone, lurched into the road from a side street, pushing Will from his bike into the path of oncoming traffic. No one expected him to survive, but somehow he battled through. He is saving up for a recumbent bike so that he will be able to get back out into the wide open spaces with his family. But, of course, none of this would have happened if the roads in his home town were traffic-free.

This is not pie in the sky. New cities are being planned and built around integrated, personalised rapid transit. Masdar City near Abu Dhabi, for

---

[26] *RAC Foundation (Mobility).*
[27] *RAC Foundation (Environment).*

example, plans to be home to fifty thousand people with cars restricted to car parks on the perimeter of the new city.[28] Some cities go car-free on the 22 September every year. Campaigners claim that over 100 million people see their lives transformed during these 24 hours.[29] And indeed the results can be dramatic. When traffic stops in Israel in observance of Yom Kippur, NO_x pollution plummets by 99% and cyclists are seen happily cycling on eight-lane motorways, enjoying the fresh air and quiet.[30]

Car-free areas in British cities are not unheard of. The pioneering 1967 pedestrianisation of Norwich city centre was originally controversial but has recently been extended.[31] Perhaps the time has come for such schemes to be rolled out across the country? Seed capital from the Department for Transport to help provide car parking on the periphery of city centres and clean rapid transit to the shopping areas could transform our towns and cities. Better still, it could transform people's attitudes to their cars. The RAC Foundation notes that cars are only in use for 4% of the time.[32] Why do we invest so much money in an object that is dirty, dangerous and idle?

It could be beautiful, and it could be your legacy. Your name could go down in history with other illustrious and fearless environmental campaigners and reformers. Or would you rather be known as the pusillanimous man who flinched when faced with the biggest question of his day, instead betraying your nation for thirty pieces of silver and a plump Parliamentary pension? Grasp this nettle now and see blossom in our lifetime a new way of urban life where smiling children play in quiet streets, cyclists exercise body and mind as they commute and decades of pollution, pain and degradation are consigned to history. We can be a beacon to the world. We can do this. Are you ready?

Yours sincerely,

Robert Ketteringham.

(President of South Norfolk Environmental Action Group)

---

[28] *The Economist*, 6 December 2008.
[29] Aisha Hannibal, *Living Streets*.
[30] Sharon Udasin, *The Jerusalem Post*, 5 October 2014.
[31] *BBC News*, 17 July 2017.
[32] *RAC Foundation (Mobility)*.

7: Writing Checklist

As you read, check how many of the recommendations below are followed by the text. Then, use the checklist to help you write your own text.

Remember that these are *recommendations* from an experienced teacher, not *requirements*. Allow them to help and guide you, but don't allow them to trap you; if you have a different idea and feel confident and excited about it, then give it a go!

☐ Clearly meets the purpose of the task.

☐ Clearly communicates to the audience of the task.

☐ Clearly meets the requested format of the task.

☐ Five to six main paragraphs.

☐ Structured to lead to a powerful 'call to action' closing.

☐ Range of different styles: descriptive, factual, emotive.

☐ Use of specific detail (avoiding vagueness and repetition).

☐ Five to seven sentences per paragraph.

☐ Sentences are varied lengths.

☐ Use of fronted adverbial.

☐ Use of extended noun phrase.

☐ Vocabulary is more formal than everyday language.

☐ Contains descriptive language.

☐ Contains facts.

☐ Contains statistics.

☐ Contains quotations.

☐ Contains a small number of rhetorical questions.

☐ No overuse or repetition of "I."

☐ Powerful, non-repetitive use of "we" and/or "you."

☐ Spelling, punctuation and grammar are accurate.

☐ Use of: colon, semi-colon, hyphen, dash.

☐ 450-750 words in total.

8: A letter about fame

You are advised to spend the correct amount of time on this section (check Appendix 1 for your exam board's time).
Write in full sentences.
You are reminded of the need to plan your answer.
You should leave enough time to check your work at the end.

"It is people who have extraordinary skill, courage and determination who deserve to be famous, not those who have good looks or lots of money or behave badly."

Write a letter to the editor of a newspaper in which you argue your point of view in response to this statement.

Space for planning:

8: The Text

Dear Phyllis Wicklewood,

Yet again your newspaper sees fit to print salacious gossip about Lazlo Wainwright's outrageous private life. Clearly, interest in the sordid details of his high roller lifestyle drives people to your publication. Corks must pop in the boardroom every time his fast cars, champagne swimming pools and gold-plated toilets catapult him back into the public eye. As a teenager, however, it only makes me sad. Sad that Wainwright's behaviour is celebrated and emulated by your misled readers. Sad that teenagers aspire to fame and wealth, preferably without doing any hard work. Sad, finally, that our true national heroes do not receive the same celebration nor anywhere near the same remuneration.

The shocking evidence of this topsy-turvy view of the world can be seen on the streets of our cities. As many as six thousand armed forces veterans have no fixed address and many of them end up sleeping rough.[33] These are the people who put their lives on the line to protect us yet we are unable to look after them properly in retirement. By comparison, an Instagram influencer recommends a slimming tea to her followers and earns more money in twenty-four hours than a struggling veteran will see in a year.[34] Meanwhile, according to the national media, the more important story is that a footballer has had a new haircut.

Take Dave, for instance, a highly skilled paramedic. It is not unusual for him to experience torrents of verbal abuse and he is often the target of physical attacks or even spitting. Dave is a hero, yet he is treated appallingly by the public. At the end of his shift, he eats pound shop pasta and avoids opening the final demands that pile up on his doormat. On his television screen, an overpaid newsreader in an expensive suit looks smug as he gets paid astronomical sums to read an autocue. We need to pay more attention, and more money, to people like Dave whose skill and courage should make this country proud.

[33] Ed Tytherleigh, *LocalGov*, 14 October 2019.
[34] Hilary Brueck, *Insider*, 6 November 2019.

Thus, as the editor of a well-respected widely circulated newspaper, you have the power, and the responsibility, to change the cultural conversation. Start today by reducing the amount of coverage you give to wealthy celebrities. Instead of printing a weekly column offering the latest wafflings from a privately educated actor with ideas above their station, commission Dave to write articles about life in modern Britain. Make sure to pay him the same as you pay the already-rich actor. Commit to reducing the number of column inches devoted simply to pictures of good-looking celebrities. How about pictures of real people in their real lives, struggling to make ends meet, striving to be happy? Celebrate the ordinary people of Britain because: we're worth it!

We can go further: an award scheme should be set up that lavishly rewards everyday heroes. There should be a presentation evening, every bit as glitzy as the Oscars and with the same amount of breathless press coverage. Attendees should receive goody bags worth thousands of pounds and, most importantly, prize-winners should receive substantial tax-free prizes. Where will the money come from? From celebrities of course. Each prize will be sponsored by a celebrity who will have to pay £100,000 to have their name attached to the award scheme. The local heroes get transformative cash prizes allowing them to buy property, invest in education or maybe to live the dream of a glamorous Caribbean holiday. The celebrities still get the oxygen of publicity they crave, and they get to look virtuous in the process. It's a win-win.

Imagine then, a changed media landscape where skill, courage and determination are the attributes held up for celebration and reward and ordinary hard-working people, striving to do their best for their families and local communities are celebrated as role models and heroes. There should be statues honouring their memory. We should take the lead of one Norfolk market town and name streets after local heroes. There they honour Ethel Gooch and Robert Kett, not Lazlo Wainwright nor his overpaid pampered mates. I urge you then, for the sake of all young people like me who feel alienated by the excesses of celebrity culture: be part of the solution and build a kinder, better, more honest culture about real people and real lives.

Yours sincerely,

Margot Vestibule.

(Head Girl, Hemsby Community College)

8: Writing Checklist

As you read, check how many of the recommendations below are followed by the text. Then, use the checklist to help you write your own text.

Remember that these are *recommendations* from an experienced teacher, not *requirements*. Allow them to help and guide you, but don't allow them to trap you; if you have a different idea and feel confident and excited about it, then give it a go!

- ☐ Clearly meets the purpose of the task.
- ☐ Clearly communicates to the audience of the task.
- ☐ Clearly meets the requested format of the task.
- ☐ Five to six main paragraphs.
- ☐ Structured to lead to a powerful 'call to action' closing.
- ☐ Range of different styles: descriptive, factual, emotive.
- ☐ Use of specific detail (avoiding vagueness and repetition).
- ☐ Five to seven sentences per paragraph.
- ☐ Sentences are varied lengths.
- ☐ Use of fronted adverbial.
- ☐ Use of extended noun phrase.

- ☐ Vocabulary is more formal than everyday language.
- ☐ Contains descriptive language.
- ☐ Contains facts.
- ☐ Contains statistics.
- ☐ Contains quotations.
- ☐ Contains a small number of rhetorical questions.
- ☐ No overuse or repetition of "I."
- ☐ Powerful, non-repetitive use of "we" and/or "you."
- ☐ Spelling, punctuation and grammar are accurate.
- ☐ Use of: colon, semi-colon, hyphen, dash.
- ☐ 450-750 words in total.

9: An article about the treatment of animals

You are advised to spend the correct amount of time on this section (check Appendix 1 for your exam board's time).
Write in full sentences.
You are reminded of the need to plan your answer.
You should leave enough time to check your work at the end.

"People protest about the cruelty of keeping animals in captivity, but they seem happy enough to eat meat, keep pets and visit zoos. All animals should be free!"

Write an article for a magazine in which you explain your point of view on this statement.

Space for planning:

9: The Text

The human animal has come a long way. From our first clumsy attempts to fashion tools to nuclear powered probes hurtling through space, we have spread into every environment on Earth, and beyond. Unfortunately, as we have shaped habitats to benefit us, other animals have seen sharp declines in their populations. Aware of this, we have built zoos to try to protect vulnerable animals, but many zoos appear to be nothing more than prisons. Meanwhile, we have intervened in the evolution of some animals to make them more useful for us, as food, as workers or as status symbols. Surely, just as *we* thirst for freedom and will fight to preserve it, shouldn't we be willing to extend the benefits of freedom to animals too?

The statistics are eye-opening. There are 235 million farm animals in the UK and farmland and urban development dominate land use, leaving only around 22% of UK land as open habitat for wildlife. [35, 36] Meanwhile, cats in the UK kill and injure around 100 million wild animals per annum and the UK's 300 zoos continue to display non-endangered animals, such as meerkats, for our entertainment.[37, 38] Our hunger for meat and our love of 'cute' animals has a huge distorting effect on animal populations, artificially inflating some whilst driving others to destruction. In fact, the WWF estimates that 10,000 species are lost to extinction every year.[39]

It was this statistic that finally changed one Cumbrian farmer's mind. Jimmy Caramel realised that he had a responsibility to change agriculture for the better. In his youth, he saw frogs playing in every puddle and barn owls swooping over the heather at dusk. Over the years, however, those populations collapsed until only sheep roamed the hillsides.[40, 41] In 2002 Caramel began a process of re-wilding. His close-cropped sheep pastures returned quickly to bracken and gorse, and trees began to take root. "I am not a prison warder anymore," says Caramel. "I don't patrol my fields, selecting for slaughter.

[35] *DEFRA*, 2019.
[36] Hannah Faup, *Full Fact*, 19 December 2017.
[37] *RSPB*.
[38] *Born Free*.
[39] *WWF*.
[40] *Cumbria Wildlife Trust*.
[41] *Cumbria Wildlife Trust*, 4 October 2019.

Instead, I gaze out over the wonder of nature where animals are free to live as they please."

Such dramatic transformations are laudable but are surely not sustainable, as long as the majority of us eat meat. Around 96% of the UK population are meat-eaters, consuming c79 kilograms per person per year.[42] "Most would prefer to turn a blind eye to the horrifying truths," notes Professor Fundenhall of Future Foods Ltd., "if it means they get a cheap plate of sausages for dinner." Professor Fundenhall's company is at the forefront of 'food futurism' and is shortly to bring the UK's first artificial meat products to market. "Weaning people off farmed meat and persuading them to consume lab-grown meat is our mission," she declares. "This could be a game-changer."

Indeed. But why stop there? In the era of 4K television, there is simply no need for zoos. Their conservation work can continue without the need to exhibit captive animals for our entertainment, and parents can be persuaded to find other things to do with bored children during the summer holidays. Then there is the tricky matter of pets. An outright ban would likely be widely flouted, so campaigners must hope instead for slow changes in attitudes as Britain shifts away from animal mistreatment as the basis of our economy. Just as smoking used to be the height of fashion but is now widely viewed as unfashionable, perhaps the practice of keeping pets will also be frowned upon by future generations who will, instead, favour wild animals born free, roaming free.

Imagine a future where Britain leads the way in re-generating our wild places, turning our farmland into a vast open habitat for newly emancipated animals, throwing open the gates of the zoos and liberating our pets. Plants, birds, insects and all manner of microbial life will also benefit from such benevolence. It will be a difficult journey but heroes such as Caramel and Fundenhall have led the way and shown just what is possible. The naysayers need to be persuaded to change their meat-eating, zoo-going, pet-owning habits and we can then look to a bright future where humans and all other organisms will live happily side-by-side, giving and taking, sharing and learning and, above all, living free.

---

[42] Joël Reland, *Full Fact*, 21 February 2018.

9: Writing Checklist

As you read, check how many of the recommendations below are followed by the text. Then, use the checklist to help you write your own text.

Remember that these are *recommendations* from an experienced teacher, not *requirements*. Allow them to help and guide you, but don't allow them to trap you; if you have a different idea and feel confident and excited about it, then give it a go!

☐ Clearly meets the purpose of the task.

☐ Clearly communicates to the audience of the task.

☐ Clearly meets the requested format of the task.

☐ Five to six main paragraphs.

☐ Structured to lead to a powerful 'call to action' closing.

☐ Range of different styles: descriptive, factual, emotive.

☐ Use of specific detail (avoiding vagueness and repetition).

☐ Five to seven sentences per paragraph.

☐ Sentences are varied lengths.

☐ Use of fronted adverbial.

☐ Use of extended noun phrase.

☐ Vocabulary is more formal than everyday language.

☐ Contains descriptive language.

☐ Contains facts.

☐ Contains statistics.

☐ Contains quotations.

☐ Contains a small number of rhetorical questions.

☐ No overuse or repetition of "I."

☐ Powerful, non-repetitive use of "we" and/or "you."

☐ Spelling, punctuation and grammar are accurate.

☐ Use of: colon, semi-colon, hyphen, dash.

☐ 450-750 words in total.

10: An article about social media

You are advised to spend the correct amount of time on this section (check Appendix 1 for your exam board's time).
Write in full sentences.
You are reminded of the need to plan your answer.
You should leave enough time to check your work at the end.

The following quotation is from an article in a national newspaper: "Young people today have become obsessed with social networking sites which are a bad influence and can take over their lives. These sites should be banned."

Write an article in reply in which you agree or disagree with the quotation.

Space for planning:

10: The Text

We are all guilty of spending too much time on social media; so much so that likes, swipes and follows are more important to us than a smile from an old friend. Worse, many use social media for ill, spreading discord and hate through misinformation, prejudice and criminal behaviour. This has led some parents, including in Silicon Valley, to try to dissuade their children from using social media.[43] A complete ban, though, would be unworkable and would deprive us of the many exciting possibilities social media offers us. Instead, we have to find a way to minimise the harm social media can cause whilst maximising the benefits it brings.

Indeed, the benefits are many. Pablo Baccata, Professor at the University of South Norfolk, reminds us that "as recently as 1996 there were only four terrestrial television channels in the UK." By comparison to today, this seems extremely limited and Baccata argues that we should not forget how difficult it was to access information during what he refers to humorously as "the dark ages." He notes that "we can fire up our phones and view stunning images of the Happisburgh fossilised footprints, communicate in video with loved ones on the other side of the world and then sell our goods and services to a potential market of seven billion – all without leaving our homes.[44] We should not throw that away."

However, the story of Mia, a teenager from the east of England, shows social media's dark side. For Mia, the glamorous lifestyle of her celebrity heroes caused her to dismiss her own small-town life as parochial and bland. Then, lost in a toxic world of 'thinspiration' and 'pro-ana' influencers, she stopped eating.[45] Her parents and friends struggled to help her, but she refused to listen. Happily, the story ends well: Mia went on a 'digital detox'. She was able to change her relationship with social media and she became healthy again. Now, she cares less about what a faceless 'fan' in Idaho thinks and looks instead to her family and friends for support and love.

[43] Chris Weller, *Business Insider*, 18 February 2018.
[44] *Natural History Museum*, 7 February 2014.
[45] Lindsay Dodgson, *Insider*, 15 May 2019.

It's easy, then, to be dismissive of social media, especially if we think of it only in terms of cat videos and trolling. However, in some parts of the world where the traditional media is tightly controlled by authoritarian regimes, social media can be a vital tool for dissidents who find ways to use messaging apps and image sharing services to get their messages out. VPNs (virtual private networks) that mask the location of the user reduce some of the risk of being caught. Unfortunately, authoritarian regimes are willing to find and destroy these dissidents every time they poke their heads above the parapet. Thus, there will always be a need for agitators for liberty and we should be careful not to remove social media from the hands of brave people who seek freedom.

Social media's myriad benefits are clear, but its drawbacks are manifold. What is the way through this tangle? The answer is an old one: moderation.[46] We need to re-learn the joys of having just the right amount of something. This 'Goldilocks principle' applies in fact to all our human behaviour. Just as we need to learn how to have just the right amount of salt in our diets so we should find ways to define how much social media is too much. One simple principle is to limit connections on social media to real friends and family, the people who really love you who will be able to give you all the affirmation you need. Thus, we might be able to sidestep all the problems of social media without seeking a complete ban.

Imagine a culture where we put down our phones and re-join the real world of real people who know us and love us. We can speak to them, learn from them, understand them. We can connect to the people in our local communities, people from different backgrounds and of different ages with completely different life experiences. The empathy we have for one another that is vital for a community to thrive will grow and flourish. We will rediscover then the joys of living in this amazing world without always wondering what an anonymous bot thinks of our new hairstyle. So, take a break from social media and don't let it control you – before it's too late.

[46] *Oxford Dictionary of Phrase and Fable.*

10: Writing Checklist

As you read, check how many of the recommendations below are followed by the text. Then, use the checklist to help you write your own text.

Remember that these are *recommendations* from an experienced teacher, not *requirements*. Allow them to help and guide you, but don't allow them to trap you; if you have a different idea and feel confident and excited about it, then give it a go!

☐ Clearly meets the purpose of the task.

☐ Clearly communicates to the audience of the task.

☐ Clearly meets the requested format of the task.

☐ Five to six main paragraphs.

☐ Structured to lead to a powerful 'call to action' closing.

☐ Range of different styles: descriptive, factual, emotive.

☐ Use of specific detail (avoiding vagueness and repetition).

☐ Five to seven sentences per paragraph.

☐ Sentences are varied lengths.

☐ Use of fronted adverbial.

☐ Use of extended noun phrase.

☐ Vocabulary is more formal than everyday language.

☐ Contains descriptive language.

☐ Contains facts.

☐ Contains statistics.

☐ Contains quotations.

☐ Contains a small number of rhetorical questions.

☐ No overuse or repetition of "I."

☐ Powerful, non-repetitive use of "we" and/or "you."

☐ Spelling, punctuation and grammar are accurate.

☐ Use of: colon, semi-colon, hyphen, dash.

☐ 450-750 words in total.

11: An article about city and country life

You are advised to spend the correct amount of time on this section (check Appendix 1 for your exam board's time).
Write in full sentences.
You are reminded of the need to plan your answer.
You should leave enough time to check your work at the end.

The following statement has appeared in an article on a Lifestyle website: "Nobody with any sense would want to live in a dirty, noisy city when they could live on a small island surrounded by fresh air and natural beauty."

Write an article in reply, which argues your views on the points made in the statement.

Space for planning:

11: The Text

Living in Britain's cities can feel like a permanent battle against dirt and noise. Our rivers are polluted, the trees are poisoned, and roads are permanently crowded as our mediaeval streets, designed for horses, struggle to deal with everything the 21st Century throws at them. Construction is constant and our cities reverberate to the sounds of pneumatic drills and the diesel roar of concrete lorries. Many struggle through life with respiratory diseases exacerbated by the permanent pall of pollution we allow to hang over our cities. Meanwhile, off our coast, lie thousands of stunning, pristine islands, crying out for new residents after centuries of de-population. Is it time, for the sake of our health and well-being, to consider a return to nature?

Part of the problem is our addiction to cars. In 2019, there were 31.7 million cars on Britain's roads and this number grows on average by 610 thousand per annum.[47] Each car pumps out noxious pollutants such as nitrogen oxides (NO_x) and particulate matter (PM_{10} and $PM_{2.5}$). Couple this with the fact that poor air quality reduces average UK life expectancy at birth by six months and you have an entirely avoidable public health crisis on your hands. According to the RAC, the cost of this pollution to human health is "estimated at between £4.5bn and £10bn annually to the UK economy."[48] There must be a healthier way to live our lives than surrounded by such dirt and noise.

Rathlin Island, off the coast of County Antrim, for example, is stunning. The air is so clear that the coast of Scotland is clearly visible fifteen miles away. Despite its beautiful, healthy setting, the population of Rathlin, like all of the offshore islands, collapsed during the 20th Century as islanders were lured away by the comforts and luxuries of the cities: electricity, education, well-paying jobs with promotion prospects. In the last decade or so, however, the tide has reversed as internet technology and a high-tension undersea electricity cable have brought these luxuries, and thousands of tourists with deep pockets, to the island. Rathlin is on the up![49] This could be the future for other islands in our archipelago.

---

[47] *RAC Foundation (Mobility).*
[48] *RAC Foundation (Environment).*
[49] *Rathlin Community.*

However, let's not be too quick to dismiss Britain's cities. It is true that Britain's cities were once hotbeds of dirt and disease where 'King Cholera' reigned.[50] Slowly, however, life improved. Drinking water became cleaner, salmon returned to the River Thames and pioneering environmental legislation, the Clean Air Act of 1956, led to a drop in pollution.[51] Life in Britain's cities became more prosperous and attractive so that young people, brought up in the countryside, yearn for the exciting vibrant life of the cities and turn their back on island life. Ideally then, there has to be some middle way whereby the beauty and health of island life and the excitement and prosperity of urban life can come together in perfect harmony.

Professor Icenorum, an expert in urban futurism, is working on this conundrum. "We cannot turn our backs on cities," he argues. "Here in the UK, 83% of us choose to live in cities and the rural population continues to migrate."[52] This is because, argues Icenorum, "cities are the motors of prosperity. They have lifted millions out of poverty." Icenorum is clearly a fan of cities then but if he doesn't recommend abandoning them, what vision does he have for their future? "In Norwich, we have a pilot scheme that shows how energy-efficient residential development, coupled with autonomous electric transportation and sensitive ecosystem restoration can lead to a dramatic increase in the quality of life." Damselflies now flit and flutter again, in stunning flashes of blue, along the River Wensum that flows through the city. "This," says Icenorum, "is our future."

It certainly is a pleasing prospect: the beauty and wonder of the British countryside plus the dynamism and wealth of cities. We could finish work at the productivity hub, grab an eco-tea from the passing tea robot and wander home through river meadows, listening to the whispering grasses and bees lazily buzzing as deer leap through stands of mature deciduous trees where once there was a snarling motorway. An impossible dream? Perhaps. A pleasant one though and certainly better than the hellscapes cities could become if we don't work hard to make them happier, healthier and more beautiful.

[50] *Schools History*.
[51] *Friends of the Earth*, 26 April 2017.
[52] *DEFRA*.

11: Writing Checklist

As you read, check how many of the recommendations below are followed by the text. Then, use the checklist to help you write your own text.

Remember that these are *recommendations* from an experienced teacher, not *requirements*. Allow them to help and guide you, but don't allow them to trap you; if you have a different idea and feel confident and excited about it, then give it a go!

☐ Clearly meets the purpose of the task.

☐ Clearly communicates to the audience of the task.

☐ Clearly meets the requested format of the task.

☐ Five to six main paragraphs.

☐ Structured to lead to a powerful 'call to action' closing.

☐ Range of different styles: descriptive, factual, emotive.

☐ Use of specific detail (avoiding vagueness and repetition).

☐ Five to seven sentences per paragraph.

☐ Sentences are varied lengths.

☐ Use of fronted adverbial.

☐ Use of extended noun phrase.

☐ Vocabulary is more formal than everyday language.

☐ Contains descriptive language.

☐ Contains facts.

☐ Contains statistics.

☐ Contains quotations.

☐ Contains a small number of rhetorical questions.

☐ No overuse or repetition of "I."

☐ Powerful, non-repetitive use of "we" and/or "you."

☐ Spelling, punctuation and grammar are accurate.

☐ Use of: colon, semi-colon, hyphen, dash.

☐ 450-750 words in total.

12: An article about holidays in Great Britain

You are advised to spend the correct amount of time on this section (check Appendix 1 for your exam board's time).
Write in full sentences.
You are reminded of the need to plan your answer.
You should leave enough time to check your work at the end.

A recent article on a travel website has stated: "There is no need to suffer the expense and uncertainty of going abroad for a holiday; Great Britain has everything anyone could desire."

Write an article, in reply, which argues your views on the statement.

Space for planning:

12: The Text

We've all had that end-of-holiday moment, standing in an airport queue, grimacing as rucksack straps bite into sunburn, when we've wondered to ourselves: and this was supposed to be relaxing? Then we check the credit card bill and suddenly decide that the family will go on a bread-and-water diet for the next month and that Netflix is an expendable luxury. On top of all that, the great cultural encounters we hoped we'd have – ancient monuments, soaring cathedrals, mournful folk song – were quietly forgotten as the temptations of sun, sangria and Eurodisco proved too much to resist. So why do it? Why go to all the uncertainty and expense when our own island has everything a holiday needs?

Tourism is a relatively recent development. Until the late 19th Century travel was hazardous and expensive. Then, the development of the railway revolutionised travel and by the 1870s it was possible to travel around the world, as Jules Verne suggested, in 80 days. The British seaside holiday reached its heights in the 1950s as families headed en masse for their annual holiday in Blackpool or Bognor Regis.[53] In the 1970s, low-cost air travel began funnelling Brits to the Costas and the now-unfashionable UK resorts fell silent.[54] However, the tides are turning as increasing environmental awareness is causing many to avoid air travel and, instead, take 'staycations'. Suddenly, UK based holidays are back on the agenda.

Asmitha Saxlingham, for example, was sceptical about 'staycations' yet, in 2019, instead of going to Tenerife, she chose to holiday on the North Norfolk coast. What a revelation! Miles of stunning Blue Flag beaches, delicious fresh food and, of course, the famous hospitality of the people of Norfolk. A hankering for city life took her to Norwich's beautiful cobbled streets. Another day she visited the Broads where swallowtail butterflies explode from the reeds and wind pumps stand stark against the sky. She thrilled at learning about the Happisburgh footprints and realising that she was walking where almost a million years ago another young woman had walked. Asmitha has already

---

[53] Ellen Castelow, *Historic UK*.
[54] Guy Alexander Bell, *spain-holiday.com*, 9 July 2018.

booked to come back next year as she's only just begun to enjoy what Norfolk has to offer.[55]

Asmitha is not alone in re-discovering what Britain has to offer. By 2018, domestic tourism was 50% higher than foreign tourism.[56] Part of the attraction is the price: the average cost for a couple to travel abroad in 2018 was £987.50, compared to £574.10 to stay in the UK.[57] This bargain is encouraging some to take more holidays in the UK: a winter city break to Belfast, for example, followed by a summer trip to Pembrokeshire. This is causing the sector to grow more quickly than the wider economy and it is forecast to be worth 10% of UK GDP by 2025, supporting 3.8 million jobs.[58] Why go abroad, then, when the benefits of UK holidays are so clear?

However, we shouldn't dismiss foreign holidays outright as the world comes alive when we are there to experience it for ourselves. Place a hand on the Berlin Wall and look up, imagining the people who were killed there in their desperation to cross it to freedom. Take a mouthful of mole poblano in Puebla and be transported back through Mexican history. Stand beneath the Great Pyramid and feel the power of ancient belief and mourn the lives of those forced to build it. These experiences cannot be replaced by a meander along the prom at Llandudno. Yet, the cost of foreign travel is beyond most and, indeed, the cost to the earth is beyond us all. A balance needs to be struck.

The future is local. Attitudes to extensive foreign travel are changing and rightly so. A short gap year trip or a cultural tour of ancient monuments can enrich a traveller's life, but we should always be mindful of the costs of such luxury and consider, instead, staying closer to home. Reconnecting with the people and places just down the road from us will help broaden cultural understanding within the UK, as people from all walks of life will mingle whilst undergoing that age-old British rite of passage: wincing whilst walking across shingle beaches and shivering as the first waves break over goose-pimpled skin. Ah, the bracing British seaside![59] Just make sure to bring a jumper.

---

[55] *Visit North Norfolk*.
[56] Niamh Foley, *House of Commons Library*, 5 November 2019.
[57] Alex Butler, *Lonely Planet*, 10 January 2019.
[58] *Visit Britain*.
[59] *Skegness Town Council*, 19 September 2017.

12: Writing Checklist

As you read, check how many of the recommendations below are followed by the text. Then, use the checklist to help you write your own text.

Remember that these are *recommendations* from an experienced teacher, not *requirements*. Allow them to help and guide you, but don't allow them to trap you; if you have a different idea and feel confident and excited about it, then give it a go!

☐ Clearly meets the purpose of the task.

☐ Clearly communicates to the audience of the task.

☐ Clearly meets the requested format of the task.

☐ Five to six main paragraphs.

☐ Structured to lead to a powerful 'call to action' closing.

☐ Range of different styles: descriptive, factual, emotive.

☐ Use of specific detail (avoiding vagueness and repetition).

☐ Five to seven sentences per paragraph.

☐ Sentences are varied lengths.

☐ Use of fronted adverbial.

☐ Use of extended noun phrase.

☐ Vocabulary is more formal than everyday language.

☐ Contains descriptive language.

☐ Contains facts.

☐ Contains statistics.

☐ Contains quotations.

☐ Contains a small number of rhetorical questions.

☐ No overuse or repetition of "I."

☐ Powerful, non-repetitive use of "we" and/or "you."

☐ Spelling, punctuation and grammar are accurate.

☐ Use of: colon, semi-colon, hyphen, dash.

☐ 450-750 words in total.

Appendix 1: Exam Board Information

The below information is correct as of autumn 2020. However, please check carefully with your exam provider as exam boards make regular changes to exam timings, terminology, marks allocations, weightings, syllabus codes etc.

In the table, each GCSE exam board is listed with information identifying:
- the paper and section of the exam where non-fiction writing is assessed
- how much time is given for completing the non-fiction writing task
- how many marks are on offer for non-fiction writing.

Exam Board	Paper/Section	Time Allowed	Marks (%)
AQA (8700)	Paper 2 Section B (8700/2)	45 mins	40 marks (25%)
CCEA (5030) (NI only)	Unit 1 Section A (GEN11)	55 mins	87 marks (17%)
CIE IGCSE A*-G (0500: 2020-2022)	Paper 2 Section A (0500/02)	60 mins	40 marks (25%)
CIE IGCSE 9-1 (0990: 2020-2022)	Paper 2 Section A (0990/02)	60 mins	40 marks (25%)
Edexcel GCSE (1EN0)	Paper 2 Section B (1EN0/02)	45 mins	40 marks (25%)
Edexcel IGCSE A (4EA1)	Paper 1 Section B (4EA1/01) (4EA1/01R)	45 mins	45 marks (30%)
Edexcel IGCSE B (4EB1)	Paper 1 Section B (4EB1/01) (4EB1/01R)	60 mins	30 marks (30%)
OCR (J351)	Component 01 Section B (J351/01)	60 mins	40 marks (25%)
Oxford International AQA IGCSE (9270)	Paper 2 Section B (9270/2)	60 mins	40 marks (20%)
WJEC Eduqas (England only)	Component 2 Section B	60 mins	40 marks (25%)
WJEC (Wales only)	Unit 3 Section B	60 mins	40 marks (20%)

Printed in Great Britain
by Amazon

59486495R00038